Copyright © 2020 by Philips Coleman Ph.d

Table of Contents

Introduction

Low-fat diets, in which calories from fat sources are cut dramatically, were once considered the best way to reduce body fat and lower the risk of heart disease and even cancer. Today, we know more about how dietary fat affects the body. Recommendations now center on promoting some fats while limiting others.

A very low fat diet is defined as one in which =15% of total calories are derived from fat (33 g for a 2000-

calorie diet, 50 g for a 3000-calorie diet) with fat calories distributed approximately equally among saturated, monounsaturated, and polyunsaturated fatty acids. Approximately 15% of total daily calories consumed should be derived from protein and =70% from carbohydrates.

What is an Ultra low fat?

A low-fat diet is a diet that restricts the daily consumption of dietary fat from animal and plant sources. In a low fat diet, 15% of total calories should come from fat, which is considered as low. Anything less than or equal to 10% of total calories constitutes an ultra-low fat diet.

The new fat intake guidelines allow saturated fats consumption no more than 10% of calories, and trans fats no more than 1% of calories, and urges to replace saturated fats with mono and polyunsaturated fats.

However, you can tweak the numbers and customize your diet plan to suit your medical condition or for weight loss as per your doctor's suggestion. Before moving to a low-fat diet for weight loss, let us look at a few facts about a low-carb diet versus a low-fat diet

An ultra-low-fat — or very-low-fat — diet allows for no more than 10% of calories from fat. It also tends to be low in protein and very high in carbs —

with about 10% and 80% of daily calories, respectively.

Ultra-low-fat diets are mostly plant-based and limit your intake of animal products, such as eggs, meat, and full-fat dairy

High-fat plant foods — including extra virgin olive oil, nuts, and avocados — are also often restricted, even though they're generally perceived as healthy.

This can be problematic, as fat serves several important functions in your body.

It's a major source of calories, builds cell membranes and hormones, and helps your body absorb fat-soluble vitamins like vitamins A, D, E, and K.

Plus, fat makes food taste good. A diet very low in fat is generally not as pleasurable as one that's moderate or high in this nutrient.

Nonetheless, studies show that an ultra-low-fat diet may have very impressive benefits against several serious conditions.

Over the past three decades, thinking about fats has changed. In the twenty-first century, all fats are not created equal. Fats are described as either saturated or unsaturated based on their chemical structure. Saturated fats are animal fats such as butter, the fats in milk and cream, bacon fat, the fat under the skin of chickens, lard, or the fat a piece of prime rib of beef. These fats are usually solid at room temperature. Exceptions are palm oil and coconut oil, which are both liquid saturated fats. Saturated fats are 'bad' fats. They raise the level of LDL cholesterol ('bad' cholesterol) in the blood. High LDL cholesterol levels are associated with an increased the risk of heart disease.

Unsaturated fats have a slightly different chemical structure that makes them liquid at room temperatures. Unsaturated fats, especially monounsaturated fats, are 'good' fats that help lower cholesterol levels. Olive oil, canola oil, and peanut oil are high in monounsaturated fats. Corn oil, soybean oil, safflower oil, and sunflower oil are high in polyunsaturated fats. Fish oils that are high in omega-3 fatty acids are also polyunsaturated and have beneficial health effects.

Another type of fat, trans fat, is made by a manufacturing process that creates hydrogenated or partially hydrogenated vegetable oils. Trans fat acts like saturated fat, raising the level of LDL cholesterol. It is found in some margarines, and in many commercially baked and fried foods. Starting in January 2006, the amount of trans fat in processed foods must be listed separately from total fat on food labels.

History of the low-fat diet

In the 1950's, an epidemic of heart disease among relatively healthy middle-aged American men gained national attention. These men all had one thing in common-high cholesterol. John William Gofman , an American scientist, was convinced there was a clear link between cholesterol and

Atherosclerosis, a cardiovascular disease in which plaque builds up inside arteries and the arteries become narrowed and hardened. This idea that there was a link between high saturated fat intake and blood cholesterol with heart disease became known as the "lipid hypothesis".

In 1955, Ancel Keys, a prominent nutritional scientist at the University of Minnesota began conducting large-scale clinical studies in an attempt to prove the "lipid hypothesis" correct. In the infamous"SevenCountries Study",

Keys recorded the associations between diet and disease rates between populations and individuals within populations.

Keys did not choose countries at random, a violation of scientific norms; he selected only those likely to prove the lipid hypothesis correct. Data was published from the United States, Netherlands, Finland, Italy, Yugoslavia, Greece and Japan because this data supported the lipid hypothesis. It was found that while total fat intake was unimportant, saturated fat intake was a risk factor for coronary heart disease.

Critics have pointed out that Keys purposefully left out Switzerland, France, Sweden, Norway, Denmark and Germany because these populations consumed high quantities of animal fats and yet exhibited low rates of heart disease. The data from these countries simply did not match the lipid hypothesis so they were excluded. Conversely, data from countries such as Chile where fat consumption was low, but heart disease was high, was also left out.

It's incredible that scientific community not only refused to denounce this study but celebrated the findings. In fact, in 1961 Ancel Keys landed a position on the nutrition committee for the American Heart Association. In that same year, the AHA began recommending that the American public reduce saturated fat and cholesterol intake from butter, fatty meat, egg yolk, and full-fat dairy, replacing them with low-fat polyunsaturated oils and margarine.

This prompted physicians to encourage their patients to adopt a low-fat diet to prevent heart disease and sent food manufacturers scrambling to quickly formulate food products to be low in saturated fat and cholesterol.

The 1980's: low-fat diet and jazzercise

By the late 1980's all health-conscious Americans were following the strict low-fat diet endorsed by the American

Heart Association. It was a time of low-fat margarine, steamed chicken breasts, and fat-free SnackWell's cookies coupled with spandex leotards and Jazzercise.

The marketing messages were clear. All-natural fats would lead to Heart Disease and chemical-laden, low-fat and fat-free substitutes created in a food science lab were something to be celebrated. Science had defied nature.

Research on The Ultra Low-Fat Diet Started in the 1930s

In 1939, a man named Walter Kempner developed a special diet, called the Rice Diet, to treat patients with high blood pressure and kidney disease.

This tasteless diet, consisting mainly of white rice, fruit, fruit juice and refined table sugar, also had surprising effects on other serious health conditions.

Kempner was only the first of many to research the effects of ultra low-fat diets on health. Other well-known low-fat proponents include Roy Swank, Ancel Keys, Nathan Pritikin, John McDougall, Caldwell Esselstyn and Dean Ornish.

In the 1930s, Walter Kempner was the first to research and document the benefits of ultra low-fat diets. Many researchers have since followed in his footsteps.

In general, a low-fat diet is one in which no more than 30% of daily calories come from any fat source. On an individual food basis, the most-widely accepted definition of a low-fat food is one that has 3 grams of fat or less per 100 calories.

Low Fat vs.Low carb Diets

Low fat diets involve restricting fat intake to less than 30% of total daily calories

High fat foods like cooking oils, butter, avocados, nuts, seeds, and full fat dairy are typically limited or banned.

Instead, you're meant to eat naturally low fat foods like fruits, vegetables, whole grains, egg whites, legumes, and skinless poultry. Fat-reduced foods like low fat yogurt, skim milk, and lean cuts of beef and pork are also sometimes permitted.

It's important to note that some fat-reduced products like yogurt may pack added sugar or artificial sweeteners.

The low-fat group lowered the amount of saturated fats they consumed while increasing the amount of fiber in their diets. The low-carb group consumed slightly less fiber, but saw an overall lower glycemic index of their diets. Both groups lowered their overall glycemic load, but the low-carb group lowered it more than the low-fat group.

Calories may still matter—although counting them exactly may not. Protein still matters. Food quality matters. But carbs and fats? Perhaps not so much. Many people find they simply prefer more of one or the other—i.e., they crave more carbs or more fat. As long as you have those first three priorities lined up, feel free to design your personal diet based on your preferences, and what you can sustain for the long haul.

Low blood sugar levels can increase feelings of hunger and cause serious side effects like shakiness, fatigue, and unintentional changes in weight

Limiting carb intake is one strategy to help control blood sugar levels .

One study in 56 people with type 2 diabetes determined that a low carb diet was more effective at controlling blood sugar, increasing weight loss, and reducing insulin needs, compared with a low fat diet

Another small study in 31 people comparing the effects of both diets found that only the low carb diet reduced levels of circulating insulin, which led to increased insulin sensitivity

Increased insulin sensitivity can improve your body's ability to transport sugar from your bloodstream into your cells, resulting in enhanced blood sugar control

Still, while a 3-month study in 102 people with diabetes revealed a low carb diet to be more effective than a low fat diet for weight loss, there was no significant difference in terms of blood sugar levels.

As such, more research on low carb and low fat diets' blood sugar effects is needed.

People lost weight on both diets, but only the low-fat diet led to a significant loss of body fat. The low-fat diet resulted in higher blood glucose and insulin levels compared with the low-carb diet. This is a concern because variable glucose levels can be a risk factor for coronary artery disease.

Type of fats

The different types of fat include the following:

1.Saturated fats

All foods containing fat have a mix of specific types of fats. Even healthy foods like chicken and nuts have small amounts of saturated fat, though much less than the amounts found in beef, cheese, and ice cream. Saturated fat is mainly found in animal foods, but a few plant foods are also high in saturated fats, such as coconut, coconut oil, palm oil, and palm kernel oil.

Saturated fats are saturated with hydrogen molecules and contain only single bonds between carbon molecules. On the other hand, unsaturated fats have at least one double bond between carbon molecules.

This saturation of hydrogen molecules results in saturated fats being solid at room temperature, unlike unsaturated fats, such as olive oil, which tend to be liquid at room temperature.

Keep in mind that there are different types of saturated fats depending on their carbon chain length, including short-, long-, medium-, and very-long-chain fatty acids — all of which have different effects on health.

Saturated fats are found in animal products like milk, cheese, and meat, as well as tropical oils, including coconut and palm oil

Saturated fats are often listed as "bad" fats and are commonly grouped with trans fats — a type of fat that's known to cause health issues — even though evidence on the health effects of saturated fat intake is far from conclusive.

For decades, health organizations around the world have recommended keeping saturated fat intake to a minimum and replacing it with highly processed vegetable oils, such as canola oil, to decrease heart disease risk and promote overall health.

Despite these recommendations, heart disease rates — which have been linked to saturated fat intake — have steadily risen, as have obesity and related diseases, such as type 2 diabetes, which some experts blame on overreliance on carb-rich, processed foods

Plus, a number of studies, including large reviews, contradict the recommendations to avoid saturated fat and instead consume vegetable oils and carb-rich foods, leading to warranted consumer confusion

Additionally, many experts argue that one macronutrient can't be blamed for disease progression and that diet as a whole is what matters.

2.Unsaturated fats

Unsaturated fats, which are liquid at room temperature, are considered beneficial fats because they can improve blood cholesterol levels, ease inflammation, stabilize heart rhythms, and play a number of other beneficial roles. Unsaturated fats are predominantly found in foods from plants, such as vegetable oils, nuts, and seeds.

There are two types of "good" unsaturated fats:

1. Monounsaturated fats are found in high concentrations in:

- Olive, peanut, and canola oils
- Avocados
- Nuts such as almonds, hazelnuts, and pecans
- Seeds such as pumpkin and sesame seeds

2. Polyunsaturated fats are found in high concentrations in

- Sunflower, corn, soybean, and flaxseed oils

- Walnuts

- Flax seeds

- Fish

- Canola oil – though higher in monounsaturated fat, it's also a good source of polyunsaturated fat.

- Omega-3 fats are an important type of polyunsaturated fat. The body can't make these, so they must come from food.

An excellent way to get omega-3 fats is by eating fish 2-3 times a week.

Good plant sources of omega-3 fats include flax seeds, walnuts, and canola or soybean oil.

Higher blood omega-3 fats are associated with lower risk of premature death among older adults,

3.Trans Fat

Trans fats are unsaturated fats produced from vegetable oils. They are commonly used in the preparation of margarine and commercially baked or fried foods.

There are two forms of trans fat - naturally-occurring and artificial trans fats. Artificial trans fats are man-made fats produced through a chemical process called hydrogenation. Naturally-occurring trans fats can be found in many animal products, including milk and meat.

Artificial trans fats are a by-product of a chemical process called hydrogenation. Hydrogenation is used to turn vegetable oils into solids to improve shelf life. This chemical process changes the degree of saturation of the fat and converts the liquid oils into solid or semi-solid forms. The resultant product remains solid at room temperature and is called partially hydrogenated oils. Hydrogenation preserves foods, making them less likely to spoil. This method is also relatively cheap and imparts a desirable taste to food.

Does Low Fat Diet Aid Weight Loss?

A low-fat diet may help you lose weight if you adhere to the dietary guidelines of unsaturated, saturated, and trans fats intake. Consuming too many trans fats from junk foods will not aid weight loss.

Fats are an important part of your diet. Consume healthy fats and saturated fats in limited amounts

Note an important fact – fats are high in calories, but calories do not always determine the "good vs. bad". For example, junk foods and zero calorie drinks may be in low in calories, but they also do not contain any nutrition and are loaded with harmful trans fats, high amounts of salt and refined sugar, and artificial additives.

You should not avoid consuming the healthy unsaturated fats that help lower inflammation and inflammation-induced weight gain.

Foods To Eat On A Low-Fat Diet

Fat

- Limit total intake of fats and oils.

- Avoid butter, stick margarine, shortening, lard, palm and coconut oils.

- Limit mayonnaise, salad dressings, gravies and sauces, unless they are homemade with low-fat ingredients.

- Limit chocolate.

- Choose low-fat and nonfat products, such as low-fat mayonnaise, low-fat or nonhydrogenated peanut butter, low-fat or fat-free salad dressings and nonfat gravy.

- Use vegetable oil, such as canola or olive oil.

- Look for margarine that does not contain trans fatty acids.

- Use nuts in moderate amounts.

- Read ingredient labels carefully to determine both amount and type of fat present in foods. Limit saturated and trans fats.

- Avoid high-fat processed and convenience foods.

Meats and Meat Alternatives

- Choose fish, chicken, turkey and lean meats.

- Use dried beans, peas, lentils and tofu.

- Limit egg yolks to three to four per week.

- If you eat red meat, limit to no more than three servings per week and choose loin or round cuts.

Avoid fatty meats, such as bacon, sausage, franks, luncheon meats and ribs.

Avoid all organ meats, including liver.

Dairy

- Choose nonfat or low-fat milk, yogurt and cottage cheese.
- Most cheeses are high in fat. Choose cheeses made from non-fat milk, such as mozzarella and ricotta cheese.
- Choose light or fat-free cream cheese and sour cream.

- Avoid cream and sauces made with cream.

Fruits and Vegetables

- Eat a wide variety of fruits and vegetables.

- Use lemon juice, vinegar or "mist" olive oil on vegetables.

- Avoid adding sauces, fat or oil to vegetables.

Breads, Cereals and Grains

Choose whole-grain breads, cereals, pastas and rice.

Avoid high-fat snack foods, such as granola, cookies, pies, pastries, doughnuts and croissants.

Cooking Tips

Avoid deep fried foods.

- Trim visible fat off meats and remove skin from poultry before cooking.

- Bake, broil, boil, poach or roast poultry, fish and lean meats.

- Drain and discard fat that drains out of meat as you cook it.

- Add little or no fat to foods.

- Use vegetable oil sprays to grease pans for cooking or baking.

- Steam vegetables.

- Use herbs or no-oil marinades to flavor foods.

Health Effects of Ultra Low-Fat Diets

Ultra-low-fat diets have been thoroughly studied, and evidence indicates that they may be beneficial against several serious conditions, including heart disease, diabetes, obesity, and multiple sclerosis.

1. Heart Disease

Studies have shown that the ultra low-fat diet can improve several important risk factors for heart disease:

a.High blood pressure

High blood pressure (hypertension) is a common condition in which the long-term force of the blood against your artery walls is high enough that it may eventually cause health problems, such as heart disease.

Blood pressure is determined both by the amount of blood your heart pumps and the amount of resistance to blood flow in your arteries. The more blood your heart pumps and the narrower your arteries, the higher your blood pressure. A blood pressure reading is given in millimeters of mercury (mm Hg). It has two numbers.

Top number (systolic pressure). The first, or upper, number measures the pressure in your arteries when your heart beats.

Bottom number (diastolic pressure). The second, or lower, number measures the pressure in your arteries between beats.

You can have high blood pressure for years without any symptoms. Uncontrolled high blood pressure increases your risk of serious health problems, including heart attack and stroke. Fortunately, high blood pressure can be easily detected. And once you know you have high blood pressure, you can work with your doctor to control it.

b.High blood cholesterol

Often, there are no specific symptoms of high cholesterol. You could have high cholesterol and not know it.

If you have high cholesterol, your body may store the extra cholesterol in your arteries. These are blood vessels that carry blood from your heart to the rest of your body. A buildup of cholesterol in your arteries is known as plaque. Over time, plaque can become hard and make your arteries narrow. Large deposits of plaque can completely block an artery. Cholesterol plaques can also break apart, leading to formation of a blood clot that blocks the flow of blood. A blocked artery to the heart can cause a heart attack. A blocked artery to your brain can cause a stroke.

Many people don't discover that they have high cholesterol until they suffer one of these life-threatening events. Some people find out through routine check-ups that include blood tests.

c.High C-reactive protein, a marker for inflammation

C-reactive protein (CRP) is a protein made by the liver. CRP levels in the blood increase when there is a condition causing inflammation somewhere in the body. A CRP test measures the amount of CRP in the blood to detect inflammation due to acute conditions or to monitor the severity of disease in chronic conditions.

One study of 198 patients with established heart disease found particularly striking effects. Out of the 177 patients who followed the diet, only one patient experienced a cardiac event (stroke).However, 13 of 21 (62 percent) of patients who didn't follow the diet experienced a cardiac event.

An ultra low-fat diet can improve several risk factors for heart disease, including high blood pressure and high cholesterol. It may also decrease the risk of heart attacks and strokes.

2.Type 2 Diabetes

Several studies have found that very low-fat, high-carb diets can lead to improvements in patients with type 2 diabetes. Diabetics did very well on the rice diet. In fact, one study found that 63 of 100 patients decreased their fasting blood sugar levels

What's more, of the 72 patients that were dependent on insulin before the study, 58 percent of them were able to reduce or stop insulin therapy completely.

Another study found that eating an ultra low-fat diet may be even more beneficial for diabetics who are not already dependent on insulin .Eating an ultra low-fat diet may have benefits for patients with type 2 diabetes, especially those not already dependent on insulin.

3.Obesity

People with obesity may also benefit from eating a diet that is very low in fat. Kempner used a form of the rice diet to treat obese patients with impressive results.In one of his studies, he collected data from 106 massively obese patients and found that, on average, they lost 140 pounds

That's not what you might expect from eating a diet mainly consisting of refined carbohydrates.Obese people may also benefit from eating an ultra low-fat diet. One study of 106 people documented tremendous weight loss success.

4.Short-Term Weight Loss

If you make an effort to reduce your fat intake, it is likely that you will lose weight. This holds true for most diets that restrict a certain type of food or macronutrient (such as carbohydrates). However, to keep this weight off, you will need to continue limiting fat in your diet.

A low-fat diet is likely to be healthy and may help you lose weight if it is still balanced with "good" fats and nutrient-rich carbohydrate and protein sources. But there are drawbacks to be aware of, most notably the change in expert advice regarding fat consumption.

Health Risks of Too Much Fat Restriction

1. Poor Vitamin Absorption

Eating a diet too low in fat can interfere with the absorption of the fat-soluble vitamins A, D, E and K. Because these nutrients are fat-soluble, your body needs dietary fat to utilize them. These vitamins are stored mostly in the liver and fat tissue and are important in bodily functions such as growth, immunity, cell repair and blood clotting. If you're not eating enough fat to bring these vitamins into your body, they will be excreted, and you may be at risk for a vitamin deficiency.

2. Depression

A diet that's too low in fat—especially essential fatty acids, which your body can only get from food—might hurt your mental health. Both omega-3s and omega-6s play roles in mood and behavior. They are the precursor to many hormones and chemicals produced in the brain. One study published in the Journal of Affective

Disorders has linked low and abnormal essential fatty acid intake to depressive symptoms. Other research shows that, because fatty acids help to insulate nerve cells in the brain, allowing these nerve cells to better communicate with one another. People who are deficient in omega-3s may suffer from bipolar disorder, schizophrenia, eating disorders and ADHD.

3. Increased Cancer Risk

Colon, breast and prostate cancers have all been correlated with low intakes of essential fatty acids. Research has shown that a high intake of omega-3s slows prostate tumor and cancer cell growth, too. If your diet lacks healthy fats, you could be increasing your risk of cancer.

4. High Cholesterol and Heart Disease

Low-fat diets also play a role in cholesterol levels and heart disease. When your diet is too low in fat, your body's level of HDL (the "good" cholesterol) goes down. This is problematic because you want your HDL level to be high to help protect against heart disease. HDL collects "bad" cholesterol from the blood and transports it to the liver for excretion. When those ratios are out of balance— and when your LDL ("bad" cholesterol) level gets too high, you face cholesterol problems and an increased risk of heart disease. Essential fatty acids, especially Omega-3s, can elevate HDL, improve cholesterol levels and protect the heart.

5. Imbalance of Nutrients—Especially Carbs

If you're not eating enough fat, then you're likely getting too much of other things, namely carbs and/or protein. This affects the overall balance of your diet, which could lead to health problems. A carbohydrate-rich diet can inflate appetite and girth and increases your chances of developing type 2 diabetes. On the flip side, a high-protein diet taxes the kidneys and liver and can lead to osteoporosis. Both cases can result in nutrient deficiencies. The key is to balance all three macronutrients—fat, carbs and protein—to ensure optimal nutrition and disease prevention (more on that below).

6. Overeating

If you're always choosing low-fat or fat-free foods at the grocery store, you could be shortchanging your weight-loss efforts. Many of these processed foods contain added sugars to enhance taste; they're often similar in calories to the original full-fat product. Research has shown that people tend to believe these foods are "freebies" and will even overeat them, thinking they're healthy or low in calories. Plus, fat helps carry flavor in our foods. It leads to fullness and satiety, which means you can get by longer on a meal or snack that provides fat without feeling the need to eat again soon.

When that fat is missing, your appetite may get the best of you.

Considering the health risks of not eating enough fat, it is definitely important to include enough in your diet daily. However, not all fats are created equal. Foods such as avocados, canola and olive oil, almonds, tuna, salmon and flaxseed are all excellent sources of healthy fats. High-fat meats and dairy products, trans fats (hydrogenated oils), and saturated fats should be limited.

Just as eating too few calories can hurt your weight-loss efforts, a diet too low in fat can hurt your health, too. Enjoy a moderate amount of fat daily with the peace of mind that you are protecting your heart, brain and your body with every bite.

7.Lack of Scientific Evidence

The 20-year Nurses Health Study, involving 80,000 women, showed no correlation between the risk of heart disease and dietary fat. A subsequent meta analysis of several studies similarly showed no association between dietary fat and heart disease or death

In the most rigorous trial ever conducted to study dietary fat, the Women's Health Initiative randomized over 48,000 women to a low-fat diet or a control group. Those in the low-fat group received intense behavior modification to reduce their daily fat intake to 20 percent of total calories and to increase consumption of grains and vegetables. The control group received only "usual" dietary education and consumed 37 percent of their diet from fat. After eight years, there was no reduction in the risk of coronary artery disease (CAD) in the low-fat group. In fact, the trend was for higher risk.

Other randomized trials have similarly failed to show a heart-health benefit to a low-fat diet. Additional studies have failed to show a reduced risk of cancer with low-fat diets, or that low-fat diets are associated with less obesity. Research is ongoing into the benefits of a very low-fat diet (less than 10 percent of calories from fat).

How to Meal-Prep Your Week of Meals:

Prepare Cinnamon Roll Overnight Oats to have for breakfast on Days 2 through 6.

Make Sweet Potato, Kale & Chicken Salad with Peanut Dressing to have for lunch on Days 2 through 5.

Day 1

Breakfast (293 calories)

- 1 serving Apple & Peanut Butter Toast
- A.M. Snack (131 calories)
- 1 large pear

Lunch (387 calories)

- 1 serving Veggie & Hummus Sandwich

- 1 medium orange

- P.M. Snack (206 calories)

- 1/4 cup unsalted dry-roasted almonds

Dinner (504 calories)

- 1 serving Sheet-Pan Salmon with Sweet Potatoes & Broccoli

- Daily Totals: 1,521 calories, 67 g protein, 153 g carbohydrates, 37 g fiber, 76 g fat, 12 g saturated fat, 1,257 mg sodium

To Make It 1,200 Calories:

Change the A.M. snack to 1 clementine, omit the orange at lunch and change the P.M. snack to 1 plum.

To Make It 2,000 Calories:

 Add 1/3 cup walnut halves to A.M. snack, add 1 cup nonfat plain Greek yogurt to lunch and add 1 large apple to the P.M. snack.

Day 2

Breakfast (280 calories)

- 1 serving Cinnamon Roll Overnight Oats
- 1 5-oz. container nonfat plain Greek yogurt
- A.M. Snack (206 calories)
- 1/4 cup unsalted dry-roasted almonds

Lunch (428 calories)

- 1 serving Sweet Potato, Kale & Chicken Salad with Peanut Dressing
- 1 clementine

P.M. Snack (112 calories)

- 1/2 cup cucumber, sliced

- 1/4 cup hummus

Dinner (472 calories)

- 1 serving Stuffed Sweet Potato with Hummus Dressing

To Make It 1,200 Calories:

Change the A.M. snack to 1/2 cup sliced bell pepper and omit the hummus at the P.M. snack.

To Make It 2,000 Calories:

Add 1 large apple to breakfast, add 1 large pear to A.M. snack, add 1 cup nonfat plain Greek yogurt to lunch and add 1 serving Guacamole Chopped Salad to dinner.

Day 3

Breakfast (280 calories)

- 1 serving Cinnamon Roll Overnight Oats
- 1 5-oz. container nonfat plain Greek yogurt

A.M. Snack (131 calories)

- 1 large pear

Lunch (428 calories)

- 1 serving Sweet Potato, Kale & Chicken Salad with Peanut Dressing
- 1 clementine

P.M. Snack (197 calories)

- 1 cup nonfat plain Greek yogurt
- 1/4 cup raspberries
- 1 Tbsp. chopped walnuts

Dinner (450 calories)

- 1 serving Turkey & Sweet Potato Chili

- 1 serving Guacamole Chopped Salad

Daily Totals: 1,486 calories, 96 g protein, 158 g carbohydrates, 33 g fiber, 57 g fat, 9 g saturated fat, 1,623 mg sodium

To Make It 1,200 Calories:

Change the A.M. snack to 1 plum and omit the yogurt and chopped walnuts at the P.M. snack.

To Make It 2,000 Calories:

Add 3 Tbsp. chopped walnuts to breakfast, add 1/3 cup unsalted dry-roasted almonds to A.M. snack and add a 1-oz. slice whole-wheat baguette to dinner.

Day 4

Breakfast (280 calories)

- 1 serving Cinnamon Roll Overnight Oats

- 1 5-oz. container nonfat plain Greek yogurt

A.M. Snack (131 calories)

- 1 large pear

Lunch (428 calories)

- 1 serving Sweet Potato, Kale & Chicken Salad with Peanut Dressing

- 1 clementine

P.M. Snack (291 calories)

- 1 medium apple

- 2 Tbsp. almond butter

Dinner (374 calories)

- 1 serving Skillet Lemon Chicken & Potatoes with Kale

Daily Totals: 1,504 calories, 84 g protein, 172 g carbohydrates, 30 g fiber, 58 g fat, 9 g saturated fat, 1,390 mg sodium

To Make It 1,200 Calories:

Change the A.M. snack to 1 plum and omit the almond butter at the P.M. snack.

To Make It 2,000 Calories:

Add 1/3 cup unsalted dry-roasted almonds to A.M. snack and add 1 serving Guacamole Chopped Salad to dinner.

Day 5

Meal-Prep Tip: In the morning, prepare the Slow-Cooker Mediterranean Stew through Step 1 so it's ready in time for dinner.

Breakfast (280 calories)

- 1 serving Cinnamon Roll Overnight Oats
- 1 5-oz. container nonfat plain Greek yogurt

A.M. Snack (193 calories)

- 25 unsalted dry-roasted almonds

Lunch (428 calories)

- 1 serving Sweet Potato, Kale & Chicken Salad with Peanut Dressing
- 1 clementine

P.M. Snack (95 calories)

- 1 medium apple

Dinner (501 calories)

- 1 serving Slow-Cooker Mediterranean Stew
- 2 cups mixed greens
- 1/2 avocado, sliced
- 1 serving Citrus Vinaigrette

Meal-Prep Tip: Reserve two servings of the Slow-Cooker Mediterranean Stew to have for lunch on Days 6 & 7.

Daily Totals: 1,496 calories, 68 g protein, 149 g carbohydrates, 35 g fiber, 74 g fat, 9 g saturated fat, 1,551 mg sodium

To Make It 1,200 Calories:

Change the A.M. snack to 1 medium orange and omit the avocado at dinner.

To Make It 2,000 Calories:

Increase to 1/3 cup almonds and add 1 large pear to A.M. snack plus add 3 Tbsp. almond butter to P.M. snack.

Day 6

Breakfast (280 calories)

- 1 serving Cinnamon Roll Overnight Oats
- 1 5-oz. container nonfat plain Greek yogurt

A.M. Snack (95 calories)

- 1 medium apple

Lunch (322 calories)

- 1 serving Slow-Cooker Mediterranean Stew

- 1 large pear

P.M. Snack (244 calories)

- 1 cup nonfat plain Greek yogurt

- 1/4 cup raspberries

- 2 Tbsp. chopped walnuts

Dinner (548 calories)

- 1 serving Sheet-Pan Balsamic-Parmesan Roasted Chickpeas & Vegetables

2 cups mixed greens

1 serving Citrus Vinaigrette

Daily Totals: 1,490 calories, 66 g protein, 175 g carbohydrates, 36 g fiber, 62 g fat, 9 g saturated fat, 1,490 mg sodium

To Make It 1,200 Calories:

 Change the A.M. snack to 1 clementine and omit the yogurt and walnuts at the P.M. snack.

To Make It 2,000 Calories:

Add 1 medium orange to breakfast, add 3 Tbsp. almond butter to A.M. snack and add 1/2 avocado, sliced, to dinner.

Day 7

Breakfast (293 calories)

- 1 serving Apple & Peanut Butter Toast

A.M. Snack (301 calories)

- 1 medium apple

- 1/4 cup unsalted dry-roasted almonds

Lunch (322 calories)

- 1 serving Slow-Cooker Mediterranean Stew

- 1 large pear

P.M. Snack (116 calories)

- 3/4 cup nonfat plain Greek yogurt

- 1/4 cup raspberries

Dinner (482 calories)

- 1 serving Honey Walnut Shrimp

1/2 cup cooked brown rice

Daily Totals: 1,514 calories, 70 g protein, 161 g carbohydrates, 30 g fiber, 69 g fat, 9 g saturated fat, 883 mg sodium

To Make It 1,200 Calories:

Omit the almonds at A.M. snack and omit the yogurt at P.M. snack.

To Make It 2,000 Calories:

Add 3/4 cup nonfat plain Greek yogurt to breakfast, increase to 1/3 cup unsalted dry-roasted almonds at A.M. snack and add 1 serving Guacamole Chopped Salad to dinner.

Eat more fish

Fish can be fatty or lean, but it's still low in saturated fat. Eat at least 8 ounces of non-fried fish each week. Choose oily fish such as salmon, trout and herring, which are high in omega-3 fatty acids. Prepare fish baked, broiled, grilled or boiled rather than breaded and fried, and without added salt, saturated fat or trans fat. Non-fried fish and shellfish, such as shrimp, crab and lobster, are low in saturated fat and are a healthy alternative to many cuts of meat and poultry.

Research has shown the health benefits of eating seafood rich in omega-3 fatty acids, especially when it replaces less healthy proteins that are high in saturated fat and low in unsaturated fat. Including seafood high in omega-3 fatty acids as part of a heart-healthy diet can help reduce the risk of heart failure, coronary heart disease, cardiac arrest and the most common type of stroke (ischemic).

Eat less meat

Try meatless meals featuring vegetables or beans. For example, think eggplant lasagna, or instead of a burger, consider a big grilled portobello mushroom on a bun. Maybe substitute low-sodium beans for beans-n-franks. Or treat meat as a sparingly used ingredient, added mainly for flavor in casseroles, stews, low-sodium soups and spaghetti.

Cook fresh vegetables the heart-healthy way

Try cooking vegetables in a tiny bit of vegetable oil and add a little water during cooking, if needed. (Or use a vegetable oil spray.) Just one or two teaspoons of oil is enough for a package of plain frozen vegetables that serves four. Place the vegetables in a skillet with a tight cover and cook them over very low heat until done.

Add herbs and spices to make vegetables even tastier. (It's a healthier choice than opting for pre-packaged vegetables with heavy sauce or seasonings.) For example, these combinations add subtle and surprising flavors:

- Rosemary with peas, cauliflower and squash
- Oregano with zucchini
- Dill with green beans
- Marjoram with Brussels sprouts, carrots and spinach
- Basil with tomatoes

Start with a small quantity of herbs and spices (1/8 to 1/2 teaspoon for a package of frozen vegetables), then let your family's feedback be your guide. Chopped parsley and chives, sprinkled on just before serving, can also enhance the flavor of many vegetables.

Use liquid vegetable oils in place of solid fats

Liquid vegetable oils such as canola, safflower, sunflower, soybean and olive oil can often be used instead of solid fats, such as butter, lard or shortening. If you must use margarine, try the soft or liquid kind.

Use a little liquid oil to:

- Pan-fry fish and poultry.
- Sauté vegetables.

- Make cream sauces and soups using low-fat or fat-free milk.

- Add to whipped or scalloped potatoes using low-fat or fat-free milk.

- Brown rice for Spanish, curried or stir-fried rice.

- Cook dehydrated potatoes and other prepared foods that call for fat to be added.

- Make pancakes or waffles.

- Puree fruits and veggies for baking

Pureed fruits or vegetables can be used in place of oil in muffin, cookie, cake and snack bar recipes to give your treats an extra healthy boost. For many recipes, use the specified amount of puree instead of oil. Check the mix's package or your cookbook's substitutions page for other conversions. You can:

- Use apple sauce in spice muffins or oatmeal cookies.

- Include bananas in breads and muffins.

- Try zucchini in brownies.

Lower dairy fats

Low-fat (1%) or fat-free (skim) milk can be used in many recipes in place of whole milk or half-and-half. (Some dishes, such as puddings, may result in a softer set.)

When it comes to cheeses used in recipes, you can substitute low-fat, low-sodium cottage cheese, part-skim milk mozzarella (or ricotta) cheese, and other low-fat, low-sodium cheeses with little or no change in consistency.

Sauces and gravies

Let your cooking liquid cool, then remove the hardened fat before making gravy. Or use a fat separator to pour off the good liquid from cooking stock, leaving the fat behind.

Increase fiber and whole grains

Consider these heart-smart choices:

Toast and crush (or cube) fiber-rich whole-grain bread to make breadcrumbs, stuffing or croutons.

Replace the breadcrumbs in your meatloaf with uncooked oatmeal.

Serve whole fruit at breakfast in place of juice.

Use brown rice instead of white rice and try whole grain pasta.

Add lots of colorful veggies to your salad – carrots, broccoli and cauliflower are high in fiber and give your salad a delicious crunch.

Foods To Avoid On A Low-Fat Diet

Junk Food – Fried foods, frozen foods, zero-calorie drinks, soda, refined sugar, and processed foods.

Protein – Fatty part of beef and pork.

Dairy – Cream cheese.

Beverages – Packaged fruit juice, packaged smoothies, soda, diet soda, and packaged buttermilk.

Low fat fruit recipe

1. Breakfast Smoothie

Ingredients

2 peaches, pitted

1 orange

1 cup soy milk

How To Prepare

- Toss all the ingredients into a blender.
- Blitz well and pour the smoothie into two glasses.

2. Lunch Salad

Ingredients

3 oz smoked salmon, thinly sliced

4 cherry tomatoes, halved

1 cup baby spinach

¼ onion, sliced

2 tablespoons olive oil

½ teaspoon black pepper

Salt to taste

2 tablespoons lime juice

How To Prepare

- Toss in the smoked salmon, baby spinach, onion slices, and cherry tomatoes.

- Add lime juice, salt, pepper, and olive oil.

- Toss well, and your lunch is ready!

3. Dinner Soup

Ingredients

½ cup white beans

2 tomatoes, chopped

1 carrot, sliced

2 celery stalks, chopped

1 medium onion, chopped

1 clove of garlic, minced

Salt to taste

½ teaspoon black pepper

1 cup vegetable broth

A handful of parsley, chopped

¼ lime

How To Prepare

- Toss the onion, tomato, garlic powder, carrot, celery, white beans, salt, pepper, and vegetable broth into a pressure cooker.

- Pressure cook for about 20 minutes over medium flame.

- Once the pressure cooker cools down, open the lid, and pour out the soup.

- Add parsley and lime juice on top and enjoy a warm and cozy dinner.

These are fuss-free and delicious food options that you can make at home quickly. Now, let's take a look at the benefits and side effects of a low-fat diet.

Some Popular example of Low Fat Diets

- 80 10 10 Diet Similar to the Ornish diet, this plan promotes eating a diet of 10% fat.

- Abs Diet Syetem for increasing muscle mass and definition by eating a high protein low fat diet.

- Diet-to-Go Meal delivery based diet that offers both low fat regular and low fat vegetarian options.

F-Plan Again, popular in the late 1980s – this plan emphasized high fiber.

- Hip and Thigh Diet Rosemary Conley's very low fat diet was very popular during the early 1990s.

- Jenny Craig Based on premade frozen meals; 60% carbohydrates, 20% protein, and 20% fat an are supplemented with fresh fruits and vegetables and low fat dairy products.

No-Fad Diet   Low fat diet from the American Heart association.

Ornish Diet   Very low fat diet from Dr Dean Ornish.

Pritikin Diet   Very low fat, high carb diet.

Weight Watchers   Dieters   are discouraged from eating high fat foods as they are high in daily points.

Conclusion

Fats are an important part of your diet. Consume healthy fats and saturated fats in limited amounts

If you are trying to improve your diet for weight loss or for better health, making healthy meals is key. Plan ahead as much as possible so that nutritious ingredients are always on hand. You can even prepare healthy meals in advance so little cooking is required in the evening when you're hungry. And remember that small changes can make a big difference. If you can't make every dinner low in fat, choose one or two nights per week to use low-calorie cooking techniques and ingredients, then build from there.